P9-CPZ-570

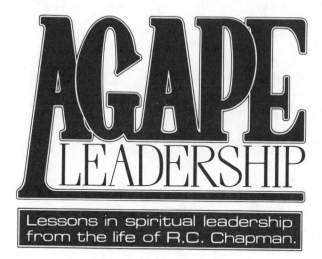

# AGAPE LEADERSHIP

## Lessons in spiritual leadership from the life of R.C. Chapman.

by
Robert L. Peterson
and
Alexander Strauch

LEWIS AND ROTH PUBLISHERS
Littleton, Colorado 80160 U.S.A.

For other books by Lewis and Roth Publishers,
write or call:
Lewis and Roth Publishers
P.O. Box 569
Littleton, Co. 80160-0569
(303) 794-3239

Cover design: Illustrated Designs
Copyright 1991

Printed in the United States of America
95 94   93   92   91           5   4   3   2   1

Library of Congress Cataloging-in-Publication Data

Peterson, Robert L., 1930-
    Agape leadership : lessons in spiritual leadership from the
life of R.C. Chapman / Robert L. Peterson, Alexander
Strauch.
        p.    cm.
    Includes bibliographical references.
    ISBN 0-936083-05-0
    1. Chapman, Robert Cleaver, 1803-1902. 2. Christian
biography—England. 3. Christian leadership. 4. Love—
Religious aspects—Christianity. I. Strauch, Alexander,
1944-
    II. Title.
    BR1725.C444P48   1991
    280'.4'092—dc20
    [B]
                                                    91-9191
                                                       CIP

# Table of Contents

Preface                              5
Agape Leadership                     7
Love for God's Word                 12
Spirit-controlled Character         18
Being Patient and Gentle            24
Maintaining Unity                   29
Disciplining and Reconciling        34
Forgiving and Blessing Others       39
Hospitality                         42
Giving to the Needy                 47
Working Together in Love            51
Vision and Evangelism               57
Self-discipline                     64
Prayer and Worship                  68
Map of England                      73

88597

*"Help, Lord,*
*for the godly man ceases to be,*
*For the faithful disappear*
*from among the sons of men."*
Psalm 12:1

# Preface

As we move to the close of the twentieth century, we desperately need examples of what Christian leaders are to be like. Robert Cleaver Chapman (1803-1902) provides an extraordinary example of such leadership—agape leadership. Although little-known today, he was a widely respected Christian leader in England during the last century. What he was best known for was his remarkable life of godly love.

Chapman was a pastor, a teacher, and an evangelist. He was a strong leader and visionary, as the results of his life's work amply demonstrate. But his leadership style did not violate God's loving and gracious principles of leading. The spirit in which God's work was to be done—not just the results—was of paramount importance to him.

Several years ago, we asked Dr. Robert L. Peterson to write a fresh, thorough biography of Robert Chapman. Mr. Peterson is a research physicist, a dedicated church elder, and a man of sterling Christian character. When Mr. Peterson had nearly completed his work, we realized that a large, detailed biography of Mr. Chapman may never receive the exposure it deserves because he is unknown to many. So we decided that a smaller book was first needed to introduce people to this remarkable man of God.

With Mr. Peterson's gracious permission, we asked Alexander Strauch, author of *Biblical Eldership,* to select choice portions from Mr. Peterson's forthcoming book and arrange them in topical order. Thus this book is not strictly a biography. It is a selection of biographical snapshots from Chapman's life that illustrate godly pastoral leadership in action. In the same way that George Muller, the famous orphanage director and Chapman's close friend, inspired thousands of Christians to pray and have greater faith in God, we desire that Chapman's life will challenge believers today to a life of supernatural, God-given love.

It is our hope that this book will touch your heart, transform your thinking about how God's work is to be done, and encourage you to be more like our wonderful Lord Jesus Christ.

The Publisher

# Agape Leadership

*"If I have the gift of prophecy, and know all mysteries and all knowledge; and if I have all faith, so as to remove mountains, but do not have love, I am nothing."*

1 Corinthians 13:2

The British playwright, George Bernard Shaw, wrote, "Christianity might be a good thing if anyone ever tried it." Shaw's sarcastic wit exposes one of our most stubbornly persistent problems—not living what we profess to believe. Nowhere is this problem more evident than in our response to Christ's teachings on unity, humble-servanthood, and love. We have failed to take Christ's example and commands seriously. Professor Michael Green, from Regent College in Vancouver, B. C., Canada, states this point pungently:

> When we reflect on the history of the Church, are we not bound to confess that she has failed to follow the example of her Founder? All too often she has worn the robes of the ruler, not the apron of the servant. Even in our own day it can hardly be said that the "brand-image" of the Church is of a society united in love for Jesus, and devoted to selfless service of others.[1]

When the Anglican archbishop of Canterbury, Robert Runcie, announced in March, 1990, that he would resign from his position, *The Sunday Telegraph,* a weekly British paper, critically remarked, "There seems little prospect of finding anyone who would do this impossible job any better; partly, it is because he is a genuinely decent person, intelligent, witty and lacking in pomposity, in a bureaucratic institution full of self-important and ruthless men.''

Addressing his own troubled denomination, but his words could be applied to most other denominations, Southern Baptist pastor Richard Jackson said, ''Get a roomful of Southern Baptist preachers together and you've got enough ego to blow Washington, D.C., off the map.''[2]

Across all denominational boundaries, religious leaders agree that the crucial problem facing churches today is a crisis of integrity. Financial and sexual scandals among Christian leaders have become almost commonplace. Power struggles and divisions are the norm, not the exception. What is the cause of these catastrophes? It is not hard to identify. As always, it is the destructive pride and morbid selfishness of the human heart. Pride and selfishness, rather than Christ's principles of humility and sacrificial love for others, control much of what is called God's work. All too often God's work becomes a matter of ego, a competitive game, or a ladder to success in the big business of religion.

How easily we forget God's command: ''Do nothing from selfishness or empty conceit, but with humility of mind let each of you regard one another as more important than himself; do not merely look out for your own personal interests, but also for the interests of others'' (Phil. 2:3,4).

More than ever before, we need to pray the prayer of the well-known, eighteenth-century evangelist, George Whitefield: ''Oh this self-love, this self-will! Lord Jesus, may Thy blessed Spirit purge it out of all our hearts!''

For those of us who seek to be leaders and teachers of God's people, Jesus Christ repeatedly insisted that we first be humble minded, that we not strive for prominence of place or reputation. He calls us to sacrificially serve one another, to forgive those who hurt us, and to treat one another as brothers and sisters in the family of God. We could summarize all these things in one word—*love*.

The love that we are talking about here is God's love, as supremely displayed in Christ's self-sacrificing love on the cross.

To express this wonderful love, the first Christians chose the noun, *agape*, and filled it with their new concept of love: God's deliberate, self-giving love that is expressed irrespective of a person's worth or merit. This agape love is to be the distinguishing mark of all Christ's followers. During the last hours of our Lord's life, He gave the disciples a new command. He said, "Love one another, even as I have loved you. . . . By this all men will know that you are My disciples" (John 13:34,35).

God's agape love is essential to the Christian life! In 1 Corinthians 13:1-3, Paul says, in effect, that if we have all the Bible knowledge in the world, if we are the greatest leaders or the most successful missionaries in the world, we are nothing if we don't have love. We are just wasting our time. Any Christian leader, therefore, who is not operating in agape love is wasting his life now and losing his eternal rewards later. If that isn't enough, such a leader is also hindering the spiritual development of the body of Christ.

Every local church is to be a display window for Christ's supernatural love. This love is to flow out of each member of the body for every other member, for the world, and for angels to see. Thus, as Paul E. Billheimer writes,

> The local church, therefore, may be viewed as a spiritual workshop for the development of agape love. Thus the stresses and strains of a spiritual fellowship offer the ideal situation for the testing and maturing [of love] . . . . The local congregation is one of the very best laboratories in which individual believers may discover their real spiritual emptiness and begin to grow in agape love.[3]

The kind of loving, mature church that God intends cannot develop, however, if the church leadership is not operating in agape love. *The local church is not to be a business, social club, or political party; it is the Spirit-indwelt family of God. Just as love is the basic element of a successful family, so love is to be the unifying element of the local church.*

For the best example of agape leadership, which is Christlike leadership, we need only to look at the New Testament letters of Paul. In 2 Corinthians 12:15 he writes, "I will most gladly spend and be expended for your souls." That is agape leadership in action!

Authentic Christian leadership involves a glad willingness to be expended for the spiritual benefit of another. Robert Chapman epitomizes such leadership. He became legendary in his own time for his gracious ways, his patience, his kindness, his balanced judgment, his ability to reconcile people in conflict, his absolute fidelity to Scripture, and his loving pastoral care.

We all talk about love, but when people hurt our feelings or disagree with us, we often immediately revert to the world's ways of attacking one another—angry debate, backbiting, and power struggles. Chapman, on the other hand, implemented the principles of agape love while immersed in the hurts and disagreements of life. Morever, his life exemplified sacrificial Christian living. He constantly gave of himself and his possessions to people in need, especially to the poor among whom he chose to live.

Harington Evans, a well-known and respected preacher of the day, described his impressions of Chapman in a letter to a friend:

> R. Chapman has just left us. He slept here last night, after preaching for me at John Street. Oh, what a man of God is he! What grace does he exhibit! Courage, meekness, self-denial, tenderness, perseverance, love for souls—all springing out of love of Christ and God—seem beauteously blended together in beautiful symmetry.

No wonder that in Chapman's day, some people referred to him as an "apostle of love." R. C. Chapman is a man we need to get to know. We may not agree with everything that he did or believed. That is understandable. But we should not allow these differences to cause us to miss the outstanding characteristic of his life—*his consistent, Christlike attitude and spirit.*

## *Thoughts for Meditation*

*" 'This is My commandment, that you love one another, just as I have loved you.' "*

John 15:12

*"Now abide faith, hope, love, these three; but the greatest of these is love."*

1 Corinthians 13:13

*"Let all that you do be done in love."*

1 Corinthians 16:14

*"Above all, keep fervent in your love for one another."*

1 Peter 4:8a

*"We know love by this, that He laid down His life for us; and we ought to lay down our lives for the brethren."*

1 John 3:16

---

*"When we would consider the love of God in Christ, we are as one approaching the ocean: he casts a glance on the surface, but the depths he cannot sound."*

R. C. C.

*" 'God is love' (1 John 4:16), His children please Him only so far as they are like Him, and 'walk in love' (Eph. 5:2)."*

R. C. C.

# Love for God's Word

> " 'If you abide in My Word, then you are truly disciples of Mine.' "
>
> John 8:31b

**B**orn in 1803, Robert Cleaver Chapman was the son of wealthy English parents. At age fifteen, Chapman was sent to London to be apprenticed in law. After completing five years of legal apprenticeship, he became an attorney of the Court of Common Pleas and an attorney of the Court of the King's Bench. Three years later, at age twenty-three, he inherited a small fortune and set up his own law practice in London's banking center. Older lawyers praised and encouraged him. A brilliant career in law seemed assured. God, however, had other plans.

During his early teenage years, Chapman had developed a strong spiritual longing that appears to have been unmet in his home environment. Some members of his extended family were strong Quakers; his immediate family appears to have belonged to the Church of England, although their religious orientation is unclear. Soon after he arrived in London, Chapman began to read the Bible—eventually reading it through three or four times. He also read writings by the biblical critics, but was not satisfied with them.

At age twenty, Chapman began to find satisfaction in his spiritual search as well as finding professional success. He became acquainted with a Christian lawyer, John Whitmore. As the two men became better acquainted, they often discussed spiritual ideas. Whitmore soon realized that his friend, who often spoke judgmentally of Christianity, was in fact searching for spiritual answers. So he invited Chapman to attend John Street Chapel, a large, denominationally unaffiliated congregation where Harington Evans preached.

For the first time in his life, Chapman heard a sermon that touched his heart. He suddenly realized the inadequacy of his righteousness and, in contrast, the great atoning work of Jesus Christ. There, at John Street Chapel, he met the Savior.

Harington Evans began discipling Chapman and took him into the slums for evangelistic work, where they distributed food and clothing to the needy. Within a short time, Chapman became very involved in John Street Chapel. Evans even gave Chapman preaching assignments, but Chapman's friends told him that he had no great preaching gift—he sounded too much like a lawyer!

His initial failure in the pulpit, however, did not deter Chapman. He concluded, "There are many who preach Christ, but not many who live Christ. My great aim will be to *live* Christ." Chapman couldn't have chosen a better goal in life, because no one brings greater pleasure to God the Father than someone emulating His Son, the Lord Jesus Christ.

A brilliant man, Chapman had many opportunities open to him following his conversion to Christ. He was off to a great start in the legal profession. Using his exceptional gift for languages, he might have been a great writer. Instead, he chose to take God's message of salvation to the poor.

So in April, 1832, Chapman left the legal profession and became pastor of a small, troubled, Baptist congregation at Ebenezer Chapel in Barnstaple, County of Devon, England. When he moved to this town of about seven thousand people, Chapman was twenty-nine years old. He had been a Christian for nearly ten years.

Ebenezer Chapel was quite different from the flourishing, peaceful John Street Chapel in London where Chapman received Christ and developed as a Christian. The congregation at Ebenezer was so divisive that three different pastors had served there during the previous eighteen months! Despite his excellent training in pastoral skills under Harington Evans at John Street, shepherding the flock in Barnstaple would prove to be a challenging task. To start with, Chapman had to overcome potentially explosive doctrinal differences between himself and the congregation.

It is amazing that Ebenezer Chapel even invited Chapman to become pastor, since he had never been a Baptist and did not share many of the church's strict views. In fact, his personal views on baptism were different from those of the membership! Given the doctrinal tensions between Chapman and the church, the situation at Ebenezer seemed doomed to failure. Chapman was sure to be the fourth pastor to leave in less than two years. But that did not happen.

What was the secret of Chapman's success at the church? He was a man of prayer and God's Word! He knew that the struggles at Ebenezer Chapel were really spiritual battles. He knew that without the Word of God and the power of the Holy Spirit there could be no victory. He knew that only the Word feeds the church and causes it to grow; only the Word protects the church from its archenemy, the false teacher; only the Word leads the church to higher and better ground.

Chapman firmly believed that unless he had the liberty to teach God's Word, there could be no ministry for him at Ebenezer Chapel. So he wisely laid down one indispensable condition before accepting the pastorate at Ebenezer. That condition is best explained by Chapman himself:

> When I was invited to leave London and go to minister the Word of God in Ebenezer Chapel, then occupied by a community of Strict Baptists, I consented to do so, naming one condition only—that I should be free to teach all I found written in the Scripture.

To their credit, the people agreed to this condition and Chapman began his life-long work in Barnstaple. Gradually the church changed under Chapman's straightforward Bible teaching and loving, patient, pastoral skills. As years passed, Ebenezer Chapel became Bear Street Chapel—a large, influential congregation of believers.

One cannot teach the Bible unless one knows the Bible.

And Chapman certainly knew the Bible! Believing the Bible to be the very voice of God, Chapman spent much of every morning reading the Bible and meditating on what he read. He meditated on the Word until it became a part of his soul. In his *Meditations*, he commented, "It is one thing to read the Bible, choosing something that suits me (as is shamefully said), and another thing to search it that I may become acquainted with God in Christ."

Chapman would not accept a doctrinal position until he was convinced of its compatibility with Scripture. He carefully based his doctrinal positions on his study of the whole Scripture, not just a cursory reading of selected scriptural portions. J. R. Caldwell records:

> Mr. Chapman chiefly emphasized the reading of and meditation upon the whole of the Scriptures. He used to say: "Every error may be based upon *some* part of Scripture taken from its connection; but no error can stand the test of all Scripture."

This intimate love of God's Word was obvious to those who knew Chapman. Someone once said, "To hear Mr. Chapman only read a psalm is as good as a sermon." James Wright, who directed the Ashley Downs orphanages in George Muller's latter years, agreed with this statement and added, "Doubtless the flexibility and skillful inflections of his voice had something to do with it, still more, his unusual grasp of the deeper meanings of Holy Scripture. But. . . .I believe the true explanation is to be found in the intense reverence for and love of the God-breathed words."

Chapman's own words best express his regard for the Bible:

> The book of God is a store of manna for God's pilgrim children. . . . The great cause of neglecting the Scriptures is not want of time, but want of heart, some idol taking the place of Christ. Satan has been marvellously wise to entice away God's people from the Scripture. A child of God who neglects the Scriptures cannot make it his business to please the Lord of Glory; cannot make Him Lord of the conscience; ruler of the heart; the joy, portion, and treasure of the soul . . . If the

Bible be used aright by anyone, it will be to him the most pleasant book in the world.

The Bible, Chapman knew, is God's sure Word and would not lead people astray. Therefore he believed that the Bible should be paramount in one's reading. Without knowing what the Bible says, it is impossible to live Christ.

This lesson is important for us all. We are all prone to neglect the Scriptures, especially in our day with the great proliferation of books and magazines. It is not enough to read religious literature or read about the Bible. We must read, study, and meditate directly and continually on the primary source itself—the Bible. Charles H. Spurgeon, a great Bible reader himself and a friend of Chapman, wrote, "It is blessed to eat into the very soul of the Bible, until, at last. . .your blood is *Bibline* and the very essence of the Bible flows from you." Chapman's blood was certainly *Bibline*.

Chapman's personal love of Scripture directly affected his teaching ministry. He had found the Bible to be the exclusive, sufficient source book for all of life's matters. Therefore, his main objective at Ebenezer was to teach the congregation directly from the Bible— something not commonly done in his day. He felt that most church-goers had received too much teaching on denominational tradition and knew too little about what the Bible said. There was, he believed, a famine in the land, "not a famine for bread or a thirst for water, But rather for hearing the words of the Lord" (Amos 8:11). Similarly, in Hosea's day the priests failed to teach the Law of the Lord to the people, so the prophet cried out, "My people are destroyed for lack of knowledge" (Hosea 4:6). Chapman certainly did not fail to teach people the Word of the Lord.

In one of his last sermons, Chapman advised parents to not only pray for their children's conversion, but to pray that they would grow to be well-pleasing children of God who know the Word. "There are so many people who are satisfied with just knowing they are saved." he said. "Tell them not to be satisfied with this. I want them to study the Word, and grow in the knowledge of God. Tell them I want them to *become intimate* with the Lord Jesus Christ."

## *Thoughts for Meditation*

*"O how I love Thy law! It is my meditation all the day."*
Psalm 119:97

*" 'But to this one I will look, to him who is humble and contrite
of spirit, and who trembles at My word.' "*
Isaiah 66:2b

*"Go therefore and make disciples...baptizing them...teaching
them to observe all that I commanded you."*
Matthew 28:19,20a

*"All Scripture is inspired by God and profitable for teaching...that
the man of God may be adequate, equipped for every good work."*
2 Timothy 3:16a,17

---

*"There are mysteries of grace and love in every page of the Bible:
it is a thriving soul that finds the Book of God growing more and
more precious."*
R. C. C.

*"Satan has ten thousand devices for drawing us away from the
Scriptures."*
R. C. C.

# Spirit-controlled Character

> *"But we proved to be gentle among you, as a nursing mother tenderly cares for her own children. Having thus a fond affection for you, we were well-pleased to impart to you not only the gospel of God but also our own lives, because you had become very dear to us."*
>
> 1 Thessalonians 2:7,8

**R**obert Chapman was a knowledgeable teacher of the Bible. Knowledge alone, however, was not sufficient to change the situation at Ebenezer. In fact, it could have been a hindrance. But Chapman also radiated the wonderful fruit of the Spirit of God: "...love, joy, peace, patience, kindness, goodness, faithfulness, gentleness, self-control" (Galatians 5:22,23a).

This beautiful blending of the pleasant fruit of the Spirit and the solid teaching of the Word explains Chapman's success. He was a mixture of the New Testament characters, Apollos and Barnabas. Apollos "was mighty in the Scriptures" (Acts 18:24). The name *Barnabas* means 'Son of Encouragement' (Acts 4:36), and Scripture records that Barnabas was "a good man, and full of the Holy Spirit and of faith" (Acts 11:24a).

Years later, Chapman wrote:

> For those who are to exercise any office in the Church—that of evangelist, pastor—it is not knowledge and utterance only which are needed; but also, and above all, grace and an unblameable [lifestyle].

18

Of the importance of Christian joy, he wrote:

Our joy in Christ speaks a language that all hearts can understand, and is a testimony for Him, such as mere knowledge and utterance can never give.

Preachers who pride themselves on their knowledge of the Bible can often be rigidly dogmatic, intimidating, aloof, or impatient with people. Some even use their God-given skills of communication and knowledge to control people and serve their own selfish ends, like Diotrephes who is mentioned in the Third Epistle of John.

This was not true of Chapman, although he admitted that he struggled with pride during his early days as a Christian. By the time he arrived at Ebenezer Chapel, however, his teaching ministry was characterized by a humble, gentle spirit. He was never authoritarian or unapproachable; he was exceptionally tactful with people, compassionate, and understanding of their weaknesses. Consider this quote by Chapman:

The figure of the mote [log] in the eye [Matthew 7] shows what skill and tenderness he has need of who would be a reprover to his brother. Who would trust so precious a member as the eye to a rough, unskillful hand?

Chapman was never rough or harsh with people. Describing him, a friend said that Chapman was "bold as a lion and gentle as a nurse." His model for handling others was God Himself. "Let us be thankful," he said, "for the kind, tender, patient way of God in training us for glory."

To a missionary friend, Chapman once said, "My business is to love others, not to seek that others shall love me." One of Chapman's many quips reveals his loving care for others: "It is better to lose your purse than your temper."

Chapman always thought of the good of others. For example, he began and concluded meetings on time, for he knew that many of those attending were servants who were expected to return to their duties at a specific time. Unlike many others of his day, he scheduled annual Christian conferences to serve the needs of those who attended rather than for the speakers' convenience. He always ended conference meetings on time to allow adequate time for participants to catch their trains home.

Chapman's kindness didn't wane, even when it required extra effort on his part. As he aged, his handwriting became more difficult to read. One day his coworker, William Hake, had to ask Chapman to read a note that Chapman had written to him; the handwriting was so bad that even Hake couldn't read it. Chapman, who had no desire to impose this hardship on recipients of his correspondence, resolved to improve his penmanship. Jesting, he once said, "I am always careful not to make the postman swear."

Abraham Lincoln once commented that any man over forty is responsible for how his face looks. Robert Chapman's face clearly reflected the joy and kindness in his heart. One of his missionary friends to Spain, Henry Payne, recorded the following story:

> No doubt Mr. Chapman's countenance, which revealed his kindness of heart, was a great help to him in securing the ear of the people. He told me that one day when he was seated in a [public stagecoach] in Spain, though he had not opened his lips, a man and a woman began to quarrel furiously in French, and at last the woman said, "I affirm that I am as innocent of that of which you accuse me as is that holy man of God sitting in the corner, who anyone can see is going straight to heaven."

Even Chapman's voice expressed his personal warmth and love, which was captured in the memory of a friend who recalled, "I can hear his loving voice even now exclaiming, 'I'm delighted to see you, yes, delighted to see you. Welcome, my dear brother!' "

A Church of England clergyman, who was once a guest in Chapman's home, offered a revealing portrayal of Chapman's kindness and gentleness even in his later years when many men become impatient and irritable:

> At last Mr. Chapman entered, a strong-built man of about

70 with grey hair, beard, and moustache, the very image of Moses; and Mr. Hake followed, taller, but more bent, old and thin, and suffering. He reminded me of Aaron, the saint of the Lord. Such a kindly welcome from both the brothers, and then I listened to know how a man with such a reputation for holiness would converse—how he would differ from other men. A baby in a young mother's arms commenced to cry lustily, and I was rather annoyed at the interruption. Both Mr. Chapman and Mr. Hake spoke to the mother with the greatest concern and tenderness, and soon her baby slept. This was my first lesson in the art of love!

For a man who never married, Chapman was remarkably effective in teaching children. His childlike, joyous disposition made him popular with children, and he was as compassionately concerned for their spiritual well-being as for the spiritual condition of adults. Describing the importance of a father's responsibility to teach his children, Chapman said, "There is more glory brought to God by a man ruling his family according to Christ, than even by a just potentate ruling a kingdom."

His friend, H. W. Soltau, remembers that his children loved Chapman's visits because they liked to talk with him. On one occasion, Chapman surprised his hostess and other guests by asking that the children sit at the table with him, while the other adults sat at the "children's table." The adult guests bore their chagrin with good humor, and the children were delighted to sit at the "grown-up" table to converse with Mr. Chapman!

As a young girl, a woman had a life-changing encounter with Chapman. He asked her, "Can you tell me, my dear, why Jesus was led as a lamb to the slaughter?" He did not provide an answer to this provoking question.

The girl had never thought about this question and later asked her mother about it. Her mother directed her to Isaiah 53:5,6, where she read, "He was pierced through for our transgressions, He was crushed for our iniquities; The chastening for our well-being fell upon Him, And by His scourging we are healed. All of us like sheep have gone astray, Each of us has turned to his own way; But the Lord has caused the iniquity of us all To fall on Him.'' The girl then understood the question as well as the answer and opened her heart to the Savior.

Chapman's teaching often had a touch of humor that kept people on their toes and alert. On one occasion, when someone asked, "How are you?" Chapman replied that he was heavily burdened. The concerned inquirer was relieved when Chapman added, ''He daily loadeth us with benefits." (See Psalm 68:19, *KJV*.)

Even Chapman's closest friends were not spared from his prodding wit. John Knox McEwen, known for his pioneering evangelistic work in Nova Scotia, once visited Chapman and William Hake at Chapman's home. On the first day of his visit, McEwen was talking with Chapman while Hake was absent. During the conversation, Chapman said, ''Mr Hake is a very provoking brother. He has been provoking me all morning." McEwen was startled to hear such a remark from a man whose kindness was well known, but his surprise did not last long. Chapman continued, ''Mr. Hake has been provoking me all morning 'unto love and to good works' '' (Hebrews 10:24, *KJV*).

In 1846, his mentor and friend, Harington Evans, after visiting Chapman at Barnstaple, wrote, ''I found beloved R. Chapman all that he ever was, and more—more like Christ, more self-denying, gentle, and full of love.''

## *Thoughts for Meditation*

*"Knowledge makes arrogant, but love edifies."*
1 Corinthians 8:1a

*"And so, as those who have been chosen of God...put on a heart of compassion, kindness, humility, gentleness and patience; bearing with one another, and forgiving each other, whoever has a complaint against any one; just as the Lord forgave you, so also should you. And beyond all these things put on love."*
Colossians 3:12-14a

---

*"Give yourself to attacking the filthiness of the spirit more than the filthiness of the flesh—pride, selfishness, self-seeking, etc.— these are the ringleaders; aim at them. Fight ye not with small or great, save only with [the help of] the King of Israel. While you are occupied in gaining the victory over little sins, great sins will be occupied in gaining the victory over you. When great sins are overcome, little sins fall with them."*
R. C. C.

*"To reform the Church of God we should always begin with self-reform. Schisms and divisions will increase so long as we begin with reforming others. Wisdom is only with the lowly."*
R.C. C.

*"If Paul had much joy in his spiritual children at Philippi, he had much profit, though little joy, by those at Corinth, who by their many evils gave him so great occasion to show the heart of Christ."*
R. C. C.

# Being Patient and Gentle

*"The Lord's bond-servant must not be quarrelsome, but be kind to all, able to teach, patient when wronged, with gentleness correcting those who are in opposition."*

2 Timothy 2:24,25a

L ike a skilled shepherd leading a flock up a dangerous mountainside to higher ground and greener pastures, Chapman led Ebenezer Chapel to higher spiritual ground.

Like sheep, people do not like to change their old, comfortable ways, even if they are destroying themselves. The established congregation at Ebenezer was no exception. It took a great deal of tact and patience on the part of Chapman to help his beloved people change. Yet Chapman, like King David, proved to be a skilled shepherd of people. Scripture says that David "shepherded them [the Israelites] according to the integrity of his heart, And guided them with his skillful hands" (Psalm 78:72).

It's important to understand that, in Chapman's day, baptism was a highly controversial issue for many Christians, not just Baptists. As a congregation of Particular Baptists, Ebenezer Chapel had strict rules about baptism. The church required baptism for membership and participation in Communion. On the other hand, believers in the Church of England or in Congregational churches who had a long tradition of infant baptism found it difficult to accept the idea of being baptized again before being accepted as legitimate members of an unaffiliated congregation.

Chapman fully understood this problem and believed that the only solution was patient, prayerful teaching of the Word of God, not exclusion from membership and Communion. Two examples will show how sensitive the issue of baptism was—especially immersion, which Chapman liked to perform in the River Taw that ran through Barnstaple.

Eliza Gilbert, who was converted under Chapman's preaching at a local workhouse, had become a faithful member of Ebenezer Chapel. She told Chapman that she wanted to be baptized; her mother, however, had threatened to make Eliza leave home if she did this. Eliza nevertheless wanted to go through with it, and the baptism took place.

Many people at Ebenezer were quite anxious for her and followed her home after the service. True to her word, the mother refused to let Eliza into the house. Friends let Eliza stay with them during this very trying period. After a few months, however, Eliza became very ill and the doctors thought that she would die. Her mother, on hearing this, relented and permitted her daughter to return home, but would not speak to her.

Once a week Chapman was permitted to visit Eliza, and the mother would absent herself during these times. Eliza was also permitted to receive letters from him, and three of them have been preserved. These are the oldest existing letters of Chapman and date from 1835. In them, he writes words of encouragement and compassion to Eliza, reminding her of God's hand in all things and that she should look to the Lord for help and strength.

Eliza eventually recovered from her illness and became a stalwart member of the congregation. Other members of her family were eventually converted through her influence and Chapman's ministry. Her aged mother also acknowledged her need of the Savior and finally yielded to Christ.

We see another example of Chapman's shepherding ability in his dealings with the Wrey family. The senior Wrey was an Anglican rector, and Chapman became acquainted with this influential family shortly after his arrival in Barnstaple. Although people of different social status did not often socialize and Chapman obviously did not share the family's theological views, his cultured upbringing and manner made him acceptable to the Wreys. After a time, one of the rector's daughters was converted and wanted to be baptized as a believer.

His daughter's rejection of infant baptism placed the rector in a difficult position, but he seems to have made no public resistance to her baptism. So Chapman made plans to baptize her in the River Taw. He also planned to baptize a young farmer, George Lovering, at the same time. Word of this unusual event spread quickly. Many townspeople came, not only to see the rector's daughter baptized, but because it was unheard of to see families from such diverse classes participate together in any event. Surprisingly, the Wrey family was not scandalized by these events. Chapman had taken one more step toward breaking down barriers between people—something for which he became well known.

Chapman's personal view was that all Christians should, as an act of obedience and public witness, be baptized by immersion following conversion. He did not, however, find scriptural evidence that baptism or a certain mode of baptism was necessary for church membership or participation in Communion. He believed that all true Christians—born of the Word and of the Holy Spirit, sharing a common life provided by the Holy Spirit—were already members one of another and free to participate in Communion. It was, he believed, the local church's scriptural obligation to welcome all whom Christ had already received, even if their understanding of baptism was different (Romans 15:7).

Despite his personal convictions, Chapman did not insist on immediate change at Ebenezer Chapel. For a time, he followed the traditional practices there. Knowing the difficulties of changing people's traditions, Chapman proceeded patiently, even when people tried to pressure him to change his course of action. For example, some influential Christians in the South of Devon County, who had learned of his ministry and wanted to be affiliated with Ebenezer Chapel, advised him to insist that the congregation immediately abandon their Particular Baptist tradition. Chapman desired the same result, but he knew that unless a great majority of the church members were behind a decision that affected such a longstanding tradition, great disunity would result.

We must make it clear at this point that Chapman was patient with people concerning this issue of baptism, but not passive. There is a vast difference between patience and passivity, and they must never be confused. Nor was he unconcerned about scriptural truths. Never! He believed that he should, as the Scripture says, "reprove, . . . exhort, with great patience and instruction" (2 Timothy 4:2b). Patiently and gently, he continued to pray, persuade, and teach. After a while, most members agreed with Chapman's view and changed their requirements.

He later described that period of waiting on God:

When sixty years since I came to this place, I waited for unity of heart and judgment among the company who called themselves Baptists; and when, by the power of the Scriptures, the greater part of them were minded to throw down their wall, we waited on in patience for fulness of unity of judgment. . . . What we now enjoy here of mutual love and the Spirit's unity would never have been our portion had any other course been taken.

How many ugly, God-dishonoring church divisions and power struggles would be avoided if only we remembered that "love is patient" (1 Corinthians 13:4) and that church leaders must be "gentle" (1 Timothy 3:3).

### *Thoughts for Meditation*

*"Take My yoke upon you, and learn from Me, for I am gentle and humble in heart."*

Matthew 11:29a

*"Love is patient."*

1 Corinthians 13:4a

*"Be patient with all men."*

1 Thessalonians 5:14b

*"An overseer, then, must be . . . gentle" [forbearing, gracious, conciliatory].*

1 Timothy 3:2a,3

———————————————

*The baptism of the Lord . . . set forth in simplest fashion His own death, and burial, and resurrection, and that of all His members. When by the Word and the Spirit of God a child of Adam is brought from death to life, that child of God is a member of the body whereof Christ is the Head, and all the obligations of the new covenant bind the members to each other. If the newly-born [person] be ignorant or neglectful . . . [concerning] water baptism, such ignorance or neglect must be rightly dealt with. But how? Not by cutting off, but by Christ-like, gentle, gracious, wise instruction; or by reproof, as the case may need. To deal otherwise is grieving the Holy Spirit, the Comforter, and doing no little harm both to the excluding and excluded, especially to the former.*

R. C. C.

# Maintaining Unity

*"Walk in a manner worthy of the calling with which you have been called...being diligent to preserve the unity of the Spirit in the bond of peace. There is one body...one faith, one baptism, one God and Father of all."*

Ephesians 4:1,3,4a,5,6a

Like few other men in history, Chapman understood the central truth of the oneness of the body of Christ. This was not just another theological tenet or theory in his systematic-theology book; he did everything he could to express the oneness of the people of God. It affected all that he did.

Despite Chapman's patient ways and ceaseless efforts to keep unity in the church, the changes at Ebenezer did not please everyone and a small group seceded from fellowship in 1834. Soon the seceders demanded that Chapman's group move out because the chapel building was no longer being used according to the original practices of the Particular Baptists.

So Chapman examined the trust deed to Ebenezer Chapel and found no provisions that required his group to give up its meeting space. The seceders persisted, however, and Chapman decided that the loving, Christlike response would be to give up the building. He viewed the situation as equivalent to giving up one's coat to someone who demanded it. No longer a small group, the congregation agreed with Chapman and relinquished their rights to the building in 1838.

It's difficult to imagine this group of people giving up their legal rights because of a few dissidents. Yet that is what the Christians at Ebenezer did! Of all the situations that a church might encounter, none tests its affections and real principles like the possibility of losing its earthly possessions. Indeed, some accuse "the Church" of being the most materialistic, self-seeking, and money-centered organization on earth. (In too many cases, that is indeed true.) But to Chapman and a congregation being schooled in the art of agape love, matters infinitely more important than one's rights or material possessions were at stake.

Without a building of their own, the displaced Christians from Ebenezer Chapel began looking for a permanent meeting place and probably met in rented quarters on Sundays. In the late 1830s, the tanyard at the end of the street where Chapman lived was put up for sale. The property seemed ideal. The lot was large—more than the congregation needed at the time—so the growing church would have room to expand. It was only a few blocks from the original chapel and a few steps from Chapman's home. Most important, it opened onto Bear Street, Barnstaple's main east/west street. They decided to buy the property, and Chapman prepared the legal documents for the transfer.

Only after the documents were completed did officials of the local Church of England make it known that they had intended to build a new parish church on the tanyard lot. Surprised by this turn of events, Chapman's group met together to pray and decide what to do. Chapman was led to Philippians 4:5, which says, "Let your forbearing spirit be known to all men. The Lord is near." In the spirit of forbearance, Chapman advised the congregation to give up its claim, which it did. Once again this small group of Christians demonstrated agape love in action.

Despite these setbacks in establishing a permanent meeting place, the vigorous, evangelistic congregation was well known in Barnstaple and continued to grow. Finally, in 1842, they purchased land on Grosvenor Street, a newly constructed street close to Bear Street. There they built a plain meeting room that initially seated about 450 people. The meeting room became known as Bear Street Chapel and later was named Grosvenor Street Chapel.

How the Christian congregation at Ebenezer responded to the dissidents and to the Church of England parish proved in the long run to be correct. Not only was God highly honored and Christ's name protected in the community, but a generation later the Barnstaple Baptists had become a strong, evangelistic group whose writings showed great respect and admiration for Robert Chapman. One Baptist publication wrote that Chapman "has baptized many on a profession of faith. A large company of his adherents meet in what is called The Rooms. For holy living, weight of character, and self-sacrifice, few can equal him; yet simple and humble as a child. He is now full of years." Surely "God causes all things to work together for good to those who love God, to those who are called according to His purpose" (Romans 8:28).

Whether at the time the Christians from Ebenezer realized it or not, the seemingly unfortunate events concerning their building actually worked out to the church's advantage, helping to create a new identity for the congregation. They were no longer the Particular Baptists of Ebenezer Chapel. They were now an "assembly of Christians," as they called themselves, creating fresh new paths in worship and evangelism. When pressed for a name, they would give "Christian Brethren." This name had been used for more than a thousand years by Christians throughout Europe who had disaffiliated themselves from the Roman Church and wanted no name other than that of Christ. These "Christian Brethren" in Barnstaple were occasionally called "Plymouth Brethren," but Chapman resisted that. The people of Barnstaple sometimes called them the "Chapmanites," a term that was deeply offensive to Chapman. In his correspondence, Chapman always addressed the congregation as simply the "Christians assembled at Bear Street."

Chapman also had strong convictions against denominational distinctions and certainly wanted to avoid using any denominational name for these Christians. The names of denominations, he said, grated on his ears:

The titles given to the Church in Scripture bespeak heavenly unity, such as the body, the vine, the temple of God, a holy

31

nation, a chosen generation, a royal priesthood. Such words set forth the Church of God as a witness for Him in the world; but the names which have been invented by men are names of sects, and declare our shame.

Chapman deeply loved the church—the whole church of Jesus Christ—not just one party or sect within it. He did not have the narrow, sectarian spirit that so many who claim to follow the Bible exhibit. One of his hymns beautifully states his love for all God's people:

> Thy brethren, Lord, are my delight,
>   I love them strong or weak;
> They all are precious in my sight,
>   The froward with the meek.
>
> I serve them, Lord, for they are Thine,
>   The Father's gift to Thee;
> The Spirit, by Thy Blood divine,
>   From prison set them free.
>
> And still the froward ones I serve—
>   Thy members, Lord, are they;
> Hold Thou me up, nor let me swerve
>   From Love's excelling way.

Chapman's heart went out to all who were in Christ's family. Whatever name they took, he welcomed them. He often preached on the topic of Christian unity. Reflecting on all the divisions that had troubled Christianity, he once said, "Unless we have a spiritual understanding of this Divine unity we cannot rightly grieve for the divisions of God's people."

Chapman understood that Christian unity has more than just a practical side; it is a profound reflection of the nature of God Himself. Thus he did everything within his power "to preserve the unity of the Spirit in the bond of peace."

### Thoughts for Meditation

*"An overseer, then, must be...uncontentious, free from the love of money."*

1 Timothy 3:2a,3b

*"Actually, then, it is already a defeat for you, that you have lawsuits with one another. Why not rather be wronged? Why not rather be defrauded?"*

1 Corinthians 6:7

*"We, who are many, are one body in Christ, and individually members one of another."*

Romans 12:5

*"Now I mean this, that each one of you is saying, 'I am of Paul,' and 'I of Apollos,' and 'I of Cephas,' and 'I of Christ.' Has Christ been divided? Paul was not crucified for you, was he? Or were you baptized in the name of Paul?"*

1 Corinthians 1:12,13

---

*"The ruin of a kingdom is a little thing in God's sight, in comparison with division among a handful of sinners redeemed by the blood of Christ."*      R. C. C.

*"Our affections should be the very counterpart of the affections of Christ and of God towards the whole Church."*

R. C. C.

*"The hearts of true believers crave a fellowship which will last—a fellowship in the Spirit with each other, because of common fellowship with the Father, and with His Son Jesus Christ."*

R. C. C.

# Disciplining and Reconciling

> *"Brethren, even if a man is caught in any trespass, you who are spiritual, restore such a one in a spirit of gentleness; each one looking to yourself, lest you too be tempted."*
>
> Galatians 6:1

A major part of the pastoral task, and often the most trying, is dealing with people's sins. Agape love does not ignore sin, for love must never be separated from holiness and justice. Thus when a member of the church continues in unrepentant sin, refusing counsel and help, the church must respond with discipline. To not respond with discipline is to dishonor God, disobey the Word of God, and fail to properly love the erring member. But church discipline often causes very bitter feelings.

Chapman found no satisfaction when a problem of sin and unrepentance had to be resolved by disfellowship from the church. He continued to pray for the offending person, desiring a restoration to fellowship. In dealing with others' sin, he cautioned, we must remember God's love toward us:

> In reproving sin in others, we should remember the ways of the Holy Spirit of God towards us. He comes as the Spirit of Love; and whatever His rebukes, He wins the heart by mercy and forgiveness through Christ.

On one occasion, an excluded member became bitter and vowed never to speak to Chapman again. However, Chapman and the man found themselves approaching each other on the street one day. Fully knowing what the man had been saying about him, Chapman embraced him, saying, "Dear brother, God loves you, Christ loves you, and I love you." This action broke the man's animosity; he repented and was soon restored to fellowship.

But not all of Chapman's efforts at reconciling people were successful. In 1845 an ugly split occurred in an influential church called Ebrington Street. Located sixty miles away in Plymouth, this large church was closely associated with Bear Street Chapel in Barnstaple and was filled with extraordinarily talented people. A clash developed between its two most powerful personalities, John Nelson Darby and B. W. Newton.

Unable to reconcile his differences with Newton, Darby announced plans to set up a new congregation in Plymouth. This alarmed many at Ebrington, as well as people attending other churches associated with it. (This network of churches, which arose almost spontaneously throughout Ireland and England in the early 1830s, is referred to as "the Brethren.")

Because of Bear Street Chapel's close association with Ebrington Street and Chapman's sincere love for the two men involved, Chapman felt compelled to help bring reconciliation. He met with Darby—and probably Newton, too—toward the end of 1845, probably in Plymouth. Urging Darby not to proceed with his intentions, Chapman cited his own experiences at Ebenezer Chapel. But Darby refused to heed Chapman's advice, saying, "I will go out and whoever will may follow me." This he did at the end of 1845.

Darby's action created two similar congregations in Plymouth of about equal size. Nothing should have been wrong with that, except both churches were at odds with each other. This caused other churches of similar belief to choose sides.

Chapman decided that he should take an active role in what was happening at Plymouth, even though his attempt at avoiding a split had not succeeded. The next best thing to do, he reasoned, would be to help heal the wounds that the fighting had created. So he consulted with several leading Christian men and convinced them that a day of prayer and confession was needed. If the people involved in the quarrel would acknowledge their attitudes as sinful, he reasoned, perhaps reconciliation would result. He sent a circular letter, dated January, 1846, to all the churches involved. It was both a scolding and a call to repentance.

Not only did many people reject the letter, they criticized Chapman for having sent it. In the minds of many, Darby had acted in good conscience; there was no reason to acknowledge sin, no need for humility and confession. Chapman had failed twice.

A year later, Darby made further, more serious accusations against Newton's teachings. Newton recognized his error and publicly confessed his wrong. But Darby and his colleagues felt that Newton's reversal was not genuine and were able to influence many others to exclude Newton and his church from their circle of fellowship. Newton recognized defeat and left Plymouth permanently in December, 1847.

But the battle was far from over. It would escalate beyond all reasonable proportion, causing untold heartache. The seemingly unending chain reaction had not yet run its course. Soon George Muller and the church at Bristol were targeted by Darby for exclusion. They were accused of sin for allowing people who had been associated with Newton to fellowship with them.

Heartbroken over the bitter division that had already occurred, people on both sides made continued attempts at reconciliation, but to no avail. A meeting of twelve influential men from all over the country convened at Bath to consider the whole issue. It is here that Chapman made one of his most famous statements.

During this meeting, Chapman challenged Darby: "You should have waited longer before separating," referring to Darby's inability to resolve his conflict with Newton and his 1845 action.

"I waited six months," Darby replied defensively.

Chapman's reply was uncharacteristically testy. "But if it had been at Barnstaple, we should have waited six years."

The meeting at Bath had no healing effect. Chapman grieved over this entire development, but was helpless to do anything further. He was reviled by some of the brothers who were sympathetic to Darby's followers. Congregations where Chapman was once welcomed now refused him fellowship. However, Darby himself defended Chapman. When some of Darby's followers tried to argue that Chapman was deficient in some doctrinal basics, Darby reproved them, saying, "You leave that man alone; he lives what I teach." On another occasion, Darby said, "We talk of the heavenlies, but Robert Chapman lives in them."

Chapman's love for Darby remained unabated. He refused to use disparaging language toward Christian brothers and sisters who followed Darby. Although some began to use less than gracious terms for them, Chapman referred to Darby's followers as "brethren dearly beloved and longed for." His sorrow was genuine. There was no sense of "good riddance" on his part. He felt no sense of relief concerning those who had opposed him and had no further Christian fellowship with him. He considered them to be his "brethren whose consciences led them to refuse my fellowship and to deprive me of theirs."

Unquestionably, this was the most difficult time in Chapman's life. The problem was never resolved; the estrangement and bitter feelings between the individuals and churches involved continued throughout his life.

### Thoughts for Meditation

*"Above all, keep fervent in your love for one another, because love covers a multitude of sins."*

1 Peter 4:8

*"Let all bitterness and wrath and anger and clamor and slander be put away from you, along with all malice. And be kind to one another, tender-hearted, forgiving each other, just as God in Christ also has forgiven you."*

Ephesians 4:31,32

---

*"Whatever the difficulties of the times, and our sorrow because of divisions in the church and a corrupt gospel in the world, it is ever open unto us to please God. If this great success of pleasing God be not ours, in ourselves lies the hindrances."*

R. C. C.

*"Humility is the secret of fellowship, and pride the secret of division."*

R. C. C.

*"Pride nourishes the remembrance of injuries: humility forgets as well as forgives them."*

R. C. C.

*"When mutual intercession takes the place of mutual accusation, then will the differences and difficulties of brethren be overcome."*

R. C. C.

# — Forgiving and Blessing Others —

> *"Love...is not provoked, does not take into account a wrong suffered."*
>
> 1 Corinthians 13:4a,5b

T he natural, human responses to being insulted or spit upon are anger, retaliation, self-justification, or withdrawal. But Christians are to respond differently: they are to act like Christ, as Chapman wrote:

To forgive without upbraiding, even by manner or look, is a high exercise of grace—it is imitation of Christ.

To be sure, not everyone liked Robert Chapman. One such person, a grocer in Barnstaple, became so upset at Chapman's open-air preaching that he spit on him! For a number of years, the grocer continued to attack and castigate Chapman. Yet Chapman continued on in his ministry and, when the opportunity presented itself, reached out to bless the grocer.

The opportunity arose when one of Chapman's wealthy relatives visited him in Barnstaple. The visit was more than just a social call; the relative wanted to try to understand what Chapman was doing. When he arrived at the house by horse-drawn cab, he couldn't believe that the well-bred Chapman lived in such a modest home in an impoverished neighborhood. Yet Chapman warmly invited him into his clean, simple home. As they talked, Chapman explained what it meant to live in dependence on the Lord and shared how the Lord always met his needs. As the relative was leaving, he asked if he could buy groceries for Chapman, who

gladly agreed. But Chapman insisted that the groceries be purchased at a certain grocer's shop—yes, the grocer who had so ve-
hemently maligned him.

Ignorant of previous interactions between the grocer and Chapman, the relative went where he had been directed. He selected
and paid for a large amount of food, and then told the grocer to
deliver it to R. C. Chapman. The stunned grocer told the visitor
that he must have come to the wrong shop, but the visitor explained
that Chapman had sent him specifically to that shop. Soon the
grocer arrived at Chapman's house, where he broke down in tears
and asked for forgiveness. That very day the grocer yielded his
life to Christ!

We can hardly begin to imagine what God will do when His
people truly love as Christ loved!

### Thoughts for Meditation

*"But love your enemies, and do good. . .and you will be sons of the Most High; for He Himself is kind to ungrateful and evil men. Be merciful, just as your Father is merciful."*

Luke 6:35,36

*". . .not returning evil for evil, or insult for insult, but giving a blessing instead."*

1 Peter 3:9a

---

*"Do we meet with unkindness from brethren? Instead of shooting our bitter words at them, let us judge ourselves; and endeavour, in love and wisdom, to overcome evil with good."*

R. C. C.

*"The best testimony that Stephen bore was his last: not when preaching and working miracles, but when he pleaded for his persecutors; for then he most resembled the Lord Jesus in patience, forgiveness and love."*

R. C. C.

*"If I have been injured by another, let me think [to] myself—How much better to be the sufferer than the wrongdoer!"*

R. C. C.

# Hospitality

*"Let love of the brethren continue. Do not neglect to show hospitality."*

Hebrews 13:1,2a

The New Testament's injunctions to hospitality are all given in the context of love. Hospitality is a uniquely practical and observable expression of agape love. What could be more contradictory than a Christian church that is inhospitable, unfriendly, and cold?

Tragically, most Christians do not realize that hospitality is not an option; it is a biblical command. That is one reason why the New Testament requires anyone who would be a church leader to be hospitable (1 Timothy 3:2). If spiritual leaders are not hospitable, then their congregations will be inhospitable and our churches will become Sunday-morning religious institutions rather than the household of God (1 Timothy 3:15).

Before Chapman moved to Barnstaple, he decided that his home there would be a house of rest for Christian workers. Although he gave away most of his fortune before he left London, we can assume that he set funds aside to purchase a house for this purpose. His two requirements for a house in Barnstaple were that it be located in the poor district and that it have several extra rooms for guests.

As he furnished his house, No. 6 New Buildings Street, Chapman made it known that any missionary, pastor, or other Christian worker would be welcome to stay at his home, without charge, for as long as he or she wished. Chapman was confident that God would provide the funds to maintain this ministry of faith. He also believed that God's faithful provision would be a valuable lesson in encouragement for those who stayed with him.

A young man who ministered with J. Hudson Taylor in the China Inland Mission lived in Chapman's home for two months, learning all he could from his host. His description of Chapman's household beautifully portrays a home that is ordered according to God's priorities:

> The whole ordering of the household had in view not only the comfort, but the general spiritual, mental, and physical well-being of the many who came there for rest. It struck me at the time as being in its arrangement and conduct an ideal Christian household. The wisdom of retiring and rising early was forcibly taught by precept and example. Love and reverence for the scriptures, and subjection thereto, formed the very atmosphere of the house. There, too, the "table- talk" was turned to spiritual ends as I have never to the same degree elsewhere known. An ordinary meal became an agape [love meal], more helpful than many a long meeting. The living was plain but good. It was recognized fully that the body was the Lord's, and should be treated accordingly. It was an ideal home for a tired or discouraged worker, or for a despondent or perplexed Christian. There one seemed naturally to be in that state of mind to hear the question and heed the exhortation to one of old: "Seekest thou great things for thyself? Seek them not." A stay there for days or weeks could not but deeply influence the whole aftercourse of a young Christian.

This is clearly the influence that Chapman wanted his home to have. While living in London, Chapman had seen many missionaries become weary and discouraged from overwork. He had a deep desire to encourage those servants of God. He wanted to pray with them, talk with them, listen to them, and provide a place of rest where they would be free from responsibility and concern over their daily provisions. He hoped that, after a time in such a caring environment, they could return to their tasks with renewed enthusiasm.

Years later, another of Chapman's guests kept a journal of his stay in Chapman's home. It gives us a glimpse of how Chapman lovingly cared for those whom God sent his way.

We all retired to rest about nine o'clock last night; for the hours at New Buildings are particularly early— breakfast at seven, dinner at noon. Mr. Chapman always retires at nine and rises at four. . . . He attends to the minutest bodily and spiritual wants of a stream of visitors, some of whom stay for an hour, some for a month; . . . it was his practice, until recently, to go round to every door and take away the boots of his guests, to clean them with his own hands. He called me at my own request at five. I was awake and waiting for his step. He put his venerable head in at my door just at the hour, lighting my candle and giving me for my morning portion: "As for God, His way is perfect." A little after, he came to guide me to a little sitting-room, where a chair and warm rug were placed beside a table furnished with a reading lamp, and just in front of a lovely fire. At six o'clock I heard him calling one of the married couples in an adjacent room, with the words, "I will fear no evil." . . . We breakfasted by lamplight at seven o'clock, and Mr. Chapman, who had prepared his own breakfast earlier, joined us at eight o'clock for family worship.

This account reveals that one of Chapman's customs was to clean the shoes or boots of his visitors. After he showed arriving guests to their rooms, he would instruct them to leave their boots or shoes outside their doors so that he could clean them by the next morning. Typically they would object to his doing such a menial task. But he was quite insistent. One guest recorded Chapman's answer to his objections: "It is not the custom in our day to wash one another's feet; that which most nearly corresponds to this command of the Lord is to clean each other's boots."

This was a small, practical way in which Chapman could serve and care for his guests. It was a marvelous example to his guests of humble servanthood. A multitude of small, practical opportunities to express loving care to one another await us all. As Chapman has said:

The strength of love is shown in great things; the tenderness of love in little things. Christ showed the strength of His love on the Cross by dying and bearing the curse for us; the tenderness of His love when He said: "Behold thy mother!" "Children, have ye any meat?" "Woman, why weepest thou?"

One result of Chapman's generous hospitality was that Bear Street Chapel became a generous, caring congregation that touched its community—as well as many others outside of it—for Christ.

### *Thoughts for Meditation*

*"Above all, keep fervent in your love for one another.... Be hospitable to one another without complaint."*

1 Peter 4:8a,9

*"Let love be without hypocrisy. ...contributing to the needs of the saints, practicing hospitality."*

Romans 12:9a,13

*"An overseer, then, must be...hospitable."*

1 Timothy 3:2

———————————————————

*"All who labour for Christ shall receive great wages for little toil."*

R. C. C.

*"What is most precious in the sight of God is often least noticed by men."*

R. C. C.

# Giving to the Needy

*" 'In every thing I showed you [elders] that by working hard in this manner you must help the weak and remember the words of the Lord Jesus, that He Himself said, "It is more blessed to give than to receive." ' "*

Acts 20:35

From the time Chapman became a believer, he began ministering to the poor. His concern for the poor continued to the end of his life. He was always keenly sensitive to anyone hurting or in need. He was a compassionate man, freely giving of his time and possessions. Chapman did not believe that such behavior should be at all unusual for a Christian and preached this message to others. As a result, the Christians at Bear Street Chapel reached out to the poor in Barnstaple. They collected clothing for the poor and at one time set up a soup kitchen in a house across the street from Chapman's house.

The Christians at Bear Street Chapel also supported Chapman on a three-month missionary tour through Ireland, which began in February, 1848. Ireland had experienced a devastating famine in the mid-1840s when disease ravaged its potato crop; millions of people had died or emigrated. Chapman went to Ireland to evangelize and comfort, and to distribute money to needy individuals and newly formed orphanages. Although the amount of money he was able to distribute was small in comparison to the great need, he had many opportunities to minister to people of all faiths—Anglicans, Roman Catholics, Presbyterians, and

Wesleyans—as he walked along Ireland's country roads.

In yet another example of his generosity and compassion, Chapman had a preaching commitment in Bristol, where George Muller lived. He arrived at Muller's home on Saturday evening, planning to spend the night and speak the next day. When Muller welcomed him in, Chapman handed him some money for the orphans. Chapman did not know that Muller had nothing with which to feed the orphans the next day, but the gift was exactly the amount needed. An assistant, who was waiting in the next room for just such a gift, went out immediately to buy bread. Muller remembered this as one of many instances in which God provided for his needs.

Chapman was personally generous as well. A friend once gave him a new coat, but Chapman soon gave it to a poor man who lived nearby. In time, his friend asked about the coat, and Chapman confessed that he had given it away. He often quoted the Scripture, " 'Let the man who has two tunics share with him who has none; and let him who has food do likewise.' " (Luke 3:11) For him, these were not empty words; he took them to heart.

Chapman and his friend, William Hake, were once visiting in South Devon and had just enough money for two railway fares back to Barnstaple. During their visit they needed to separate, so Hake gave Chapman money for his return fare. They met later, and Hake (knowing Chapman's habit of giving money away) asked Chapman if he still had his fare.

"Our Father knows all about it," Chapman answered.

Suspecting that the money was gone, Hake repeated his question as they approached the railway station. Chapman confessed that he had given the money to an elderly lady who was not feeling well and could use it.

"Well, what are you going to do now?" Hake asked with some agitation.

Chapman simply replied, "Our Father knows all about it."

As the train pulled up to the platform, a friend ran up, apologized for being late, and gave each of them more than enough money for the fare!

Another of Chapman's traveling companions, George Fisher,

tells a similar story. He and Chapman were ready to leave a conference in Leominster, but neither had any money. Although Chapman had been given some money at the conference, he had immediately given it to someone whom he felt was in greater need. When Fisher reminded Chapman that they had no money, Chapman asked, "To whom does the money belong, and the cattle upon a thousand hills?"

When they arrived at the railway station, a man on another train recognized Chapman, hurried over, handed him a five-pound note, and said,"I have had this in my pocket for some time, and am glad I met you."

As the man returned to his train, Chapman turned to his companion and asked rhetorically, "To whom does the money belong?"

Yet another friend of Chapman once saw him sitting in a waiting train car. He began talking with Chapman and, suspecting the situation, asked Chapman to show him his purse. Smiling, Chapman opened his purse to reveal no ticket and no money. Chapman had boarded the train, confident that the Lord would provide a ticket if He wanted him to take the trip. The friend supplied his need, knowing that he was the Lord's agent on that day.

An incident that occurred a few months after Chapman had died beautifully summarizes his giving character. Many people wanted to have mementos from among his possessions. His friends agreed that the fairest method would be to have his housekeeper decide how his personal possessions would be distributed. His desk, chair, clothes, and personal effects were distributed in this way.

One man who had helped Chapman during his last decade told an associate about the memento he had received—one of Chapman's nightgowns. A few months after he had received it, he had tried unsuccessfully to find it to show to someone and to reminisce. After some thought, he realized what had happened. He had placed the nightgown on a pile of clothing that had been set aside to be taken to a missionary station in Rhodesia. That box of clothing had been given to one of the natives. As he pictured a happy man wearing that treasure, he said, "Mr. Chapman would've liked that!"

## *Thoughts for Meditation*

*"Sell your possessions and give to charity; make yourselves purses which do not wear out, an unfailing treasure in heaven."*

Luke 12:33

*"Whoever has the world's goods, and beholds his brother in need and closes his heart against him, how does the love of God abide in him?"*

1 John 3:17

*"They only asked us to remember the poor—the very thing I [Paul] also was eager to do."*

Galatians 2:10

—————————————

*"Though Christ can be grieved at a thousand things in us that no eye but His can see, yet none [is] so easily pleased as He by our little endeavours of love."*

R. C. C.

*"The lonely, the mournful, the friendless, the tempted, the defected, the despised, the forsaken, the outcast, Christ will wait on each one of them, whatever his case, as though that one were His only charge. By this exact and special oversight of each member of His body, how precious, how lovely, how glorious, does Christ appear!"*

R. C. C.

# —— Working Together in Love ——

> *"The overseer must be above reproach as God's steward, not self-willed."*
>
> Titus 1:7a

T he true quality of our love is exposed by the stresses and strains of our relationships with others, especially those with whom we work the closest.

Chapman was never a one-man show or a glory seeker. He was not a loner pastor. He once wrote, "We need one another; are dependent on one another—not as fountains, but as channels of blessing." Right from the start, Chapman dearly valued shared leadership. Before going to Barnstaple, Chapman asked his friend, William Hake, to join him in his ministry efforts there, but Hake could not do so at that time.

As the church matured, Chapman became one among a body of pastor-elders who taught and governed the church together. Among the elders, however, Chapman stood out in the same way Peter stood out among the Twelve, as first among equals and the spokesman for the group.

Chapman also refused any clerical title or status for himself. He firmly believed, as he often preached, that Christ was the Head of the congregation and that He was always present as Chief Shepherd to guide and protect the flock. Thus he and the other elders viewed themselves as undershepherds of Christ, their Leader. Hence, prayer was a major responsibility of the congregation's ministry, because prayer was the means by which they could know the Chief Pastor's will.

51

Like a good shepherd, Chapman was always seeking people out, pushing them forward, and helping them develop their gifts. "The Church, the body of Christ," he said, "cannot rise above its present low estate until there be a conscience in the members of fulfilling each one his office in the body." He also believed strongly that it was his responsibility to help people develop their faith in the Lord.

At that time, churches rarely provided formal training in spiritual leadership. So those who desired to teach God's Word learned "on the job." Just as Chapman had first begun preaching under the guidance of Harington Evans at John Street Chapel in London, so Chapman helped the men at Ebenezer develop their preaching, pastoral, and evangelistic skills. "To make a good soldier," said Chapman, "put him in the front of the battle; a good seaman, let him have the stern. So with the Christian."

Two young men in their twenties—William Bowden, one of Chapman's early converts, and George Beer—showed particular promise. Chapman encouraged these men to begin open-air preaching. They first did this in the slum area near Chapman's home. There, they received much abuse and threats of physical violence. But many people received Christ through their efforts, which strengthened their conviction that God had called them into evangelistic ministry.

These two friends continued to work together, preaching and evangelizing in villages near Barnstaple. As a result, small house churches were established in several villages. Some of the congregations even grew large enough to erect buildings and adopt a regular schedule of meetings. These churches depended on Bowden, Beer, Chapman, and others for pastoral care.

The pastoral assistance Bowden and Beer offered to Chapman, however, did not last long. In 1835, Anthony Norris Groves returned to England after enduring five incredibly difficult years of missionary work in Baghdad. His work had produced little fruit. Although greatly discouraged, he was determined to continue in missionary service. Hearing that there was an open door for missionary work in India, he visited there and learned that India was indeed open to the gospel. India only lacked workers to carry the

Good News. Immediately he began recruiting men and women who were willing to establish a missionary outreach in India. Bowden and Beer, and their wives, were among those whom Groves recruited for service in India.

Chapman was not at all discouraged by the loss of Bowden and Beer to God's work in Barnstaple. God, he knew, had prepared these young men; they were ready and eager to embark on their life's work. So Chapman fully supported and encouraged them to pursue God's calling. Moving on to another arena of service, he knew, was simply another part of God's plan.

Chapman helped many others, such as the young farmer, George Lovering, who Chapman had baptized along with the Wrey daughter. Lovering soon became actively involved in evangelization near Barnstaple. He later worked for thirty years in North Devon, establishing churches in several villages to the south and east of Barnstaple. There was also Henry Heath, a keen young man studying for holy orders in the Anglican Church who Chapman touched for Christ. He, too, became a leader and teacher at Bear Street and later left to preach at Hackney on the north side of London.

One of Chapman's most faithful colaborers was Elizabeth Paget, or "Bessie" as she was called. Elizabeth was twenty years older than Chapman. In her fifties, she moved to Barnstaple to devote the rest of her life to Bear Street Chapel. Although a lady of means, she bought a house in the poor district, at No. 9 New Buildings Street, across from Chapman's home.

Like Chapman, Elizabeth was an energetic evangelist. She initiated a Sunday school for children, opened a soup kitchen in her home, and also opened her home—just as Chapman had—to the Lord's workers who were visiting in the area or who needed a quiet retreat. Between the two houses, as many as twenty guests at a time were in residence.

For nearly thirty years, until her death in 1863 at eighty years of age, Elizabeth worked closely with Chapman. This is significant because Elizabeth was strong, intelligent, and a natural leader. Because of her strong personality, she and Chapman could have experienced conflict during those years. But godly humility and

love allowed them to work together in peace and harmony. Today, as in their day, such unity and peace honors God and demon-
strates to the world the power of the Holy Spirit.

Among Chapman's fellow colleagues, William Hake stands
out indisputably as Chapman's best-loved friend. Chapman felt
that he had more in common with Hake than with anyone else he
had ever met: "Our hearts were presently knit together in the
fellowship of the Spirit. . . . Each found the other a lover of the
Scriptures, and bent upon obedience to the Lord without reserve."

When Chapman first moved to Barnstaple, he wanted Hake
to join him so that they could work together in pastoring the church
there. Hake, however, was raising a young family and had a worth-
while ministry as headmaster of a Christian boarding school. He
did not believe that it was God's will to work with Chapman in
Barnstaple until nearly thirty years later. Then the two men worked
together for twenty-five years, until Hake's death. Together, they
systematically visited nearly every home in Barnstaple, conducted
home Bible studies, opened their separate homes to missionaries,
and helped the many smaller churches growing around Barnstaple.
They had such an impact on the people of Barnstaple that townspeople often referred to them as "The Patriarchs."

After Hake's death, Chapman wrote that they had experienced
over fifty years of loving harmony together in God's work:

> Our fellowship has been ever growing, and during its fifty-
> nine years' continuance, never was strife or bitterness between
> us. The dear departed one was wont to say, "Ah! dear brother,
> we never had a jar." . . . Thus we daily contributed each to
> the other's treasure of grace and truth. . . . Touching the
> guidance of our steps, the ordering of our ways, the rule of
> our household, we always waited on God together for His
> mind. . . . If judgment did not agree, we waited on God to
> give us oneness of mind, and neither of us ever took a step
> against the judgment of the other—hence no strife, no bitterness!

Chapman's statement shows that both of them did not totally
agree on everything, including the interpretation of certain
prophecies. Chapman maintained a "post-tribulational" view of

the Rapture of the church, while Hake (and most of their friends) held a different position. But their Christlike love for one another overshadowed all such disagreements.

In fact, Chapman would not allow his view on the time of Christ's return to cause division in the church. He demonstrated his humble and submissive spirit by submitting to the other elders on this point of disagreement. In 1896, he called the elders at Bear Street together "to explain that I shall not create dissension by teaching the opposite view in the assembly." For the sake of unity, he would not teach against the position of the other elders; yet he saw no need to change his interpretation.

Concerning essential doctrines and scriptural principles, however, Chapman remained firm. He carefully and boldly preached on such subjects, but balanced his teaching with godly understanding and love. Chapman's long life was marked by many rich, long-term friendships among a wide range of people. Such a rewarding life is the result of "the wisdom from above [that] is first pure, then peaceable, gentle, reasonable, full of mercy and good fruits" (James 3:17).

### Thoughts for Meditation

*"They love the place of honor. . .and being called by men, Rabbi. But do not be called Rabbi; . . .for One is your Leader, that is, Christ. But the greatest among you shall be your servant."*
Matthew 23:6a,7b,8a,10b,11

*"Not that we lord it over your faith, but are workers with you for your joy; for in your faith you are standing firm."*
2 Corinthians 1:24

*Therefore, I exhort the elders among you. . .shepherd [pastor] the flock of God among you. . .nor yet as lording it over those allotted to your charge, but proving to be examples to the flock."*
1 Peter 5:1a,2a,3

---

*"How great victory was that which Jonathan must have gained over himself, when he rejoiced to see David raised above him! He discerned the mind of God in David, and had so learnt to delight in God, that he did not see in David one who was to outshine him, but another faithful man raised up for God and for Israel."*
R. C. C.

# Vision and Evangelism

*"I am not ashamed of the gospel, for it is the power of God for salvation."*

Romans 1:16a

To have God's heartbeat is to have deep, sincere love for the lost. From his earliest days as a believer, Robert Chapman was an enthusiastic evangelist. He openly shared the gospel with anyone who would listen—friends, family, and people he met on the street. While living in London, Chapman regularly visited the poor, sharing the truth of Christ's love and displaying that love through generous acts of kindness.

When Chapman moved to Barnstaple, his evangelistic heart did not skip a beat. He immediately began tireless visitation and evangelization. He talked with people on the streets and visited with others at their houses. He held gospel meetings at the workhouses, afterwards talking personally with anyone who wanted to hear more. He also walked great distances, striking up conversations with people he met along the way.

As Bear Street Chapel grew and a strong core of mature believers became established within the congregation, another part of God's plan for Chapman's life unfolded. His heart had long been burdened for missionary work in Spain. He had no idea how or when he could go to Spain, but he believed that he would someday minister there. His first opportunity to do so came in 1838.

At that time, Spain was a very dangerous place for evangelicals. The country was controlled by Roman Catholicism. Laws prohibited preaching outside the Roman Catholic system.

Evangelicals were openly persecuted; foreign missionaries were not allowed. Chapman's friends urged him to abandon his plans, but he was determined to go. His youthful zeal for mission work in Spain had matured into full confidence that God had called him to accomplish this work.

Knowing that public preaching would be impossible, Chapman planned to use his gift of interacting with people to talk with individuals he met along the way. He was well prepared for this venture. Years before, he had studied Spanish and Portuguese and could speak both languages fluently. (Chapman was able to preach in five languages.) Believing that the time was right, he went to Spain.

During his visit, Chapman walked through parts of Spain, sharing Christ with those he met. As he had expected, the spiritual state of the country was low and open evangelism was dangerous. Near the end of his journey, as he approached Spain's Atlantic coast, he climbed the tall mountain, El Castilo. From its summit, he surveyed the country that had experienced such blessing at the beginning of the Christian era, but had more recently been the site of the Inquisition. There he prayed for God's intervention in Spain, asking Him to allow the light of the gospel to penetrate the country's spiritual darkness.

His journey over, Chapman's burden for Spain did not diminish. In his sermons he often emphasized Spain's spiritual need and urged listeners to consider devoting their lives to God's service in that country. The stories he told about his experiences stirred the hearts of many Christians in England. A number of men and women responded and devoted their lives to missionary work in Spain. During the 1840s and 1850s, several organizations also were formed to carry the gospel to Spain. Gradually the British and Foreign Bible Society (with which Chapman was affiliated) began making progress in distributing Bibles and literature there.

Chapman made two additional missionary journeys through Spain—the final one in 1871 when he was sixty-eight years old. For ten months, he crisscrossed that nation, sharing the gospel with everyone who would listen.

For part of his journey, Chapman traveled by train with a small party of missionaries. The journey was slow, with many stops. Every time the train pulled into a station, Chapman and his party took advantage of the situation and distributed Gospels. At one station, the railway inspector felt that they were overstepping their bounds since the train and station were private property.

Soon the police arrived to take Chapman and his party before the town mayor. Chapman, however, used a tactic that Jesus had used in His confrontations with the Pharisees and the scribes. He took money from his purse and asked, "Have I a right to throw this to the poor who beg at the station? Here is bread; have I a right to give this also?" The police didn't know how to respond, so they allowed the missionaries to continue their journey.

Later that night, the group got off the train to find lodging. They soon found a place to stay, but the baggage handlers warned them—for they obviously were English and religious—that the landlord was a violent-tempered, political zealot who had participated in a recent uprising. They advised that it would be dangerous to discuss religion with him.

Chapman listened, then sought out the landlord and stated, "There is one thing which English and Spanish people need more than anything else."

"What's that?" asked the landlord.

"Peace with God. Have you that peace, my friend? I have had that peace through our Lord Jesus Christ for many years."

Surprisingly, the landlord responded favorably. He asked for some Gospels that he had seen the group distribute, which the missionaries gladly supplied.

On another segment of his journey, Chapman was traveling by stagecoach. A man who proved to be a pioneer representative of a missionary society was seated next to him. The representative saw Chapman reading his Bible and tells the following story about their time together.

I soon introduced myself, and quickly found out that we were on the same errand. And as I had traveled far and wide in many lands, I proffered my services as traveling companion. Mr. Chapman at once expressed his thanks and handed me his purse; this greatly took me by surprise, and I thought I was in the company of a very good man, but [one] a little "touched in his upper story."

On our arrival in Seville, we were surrounded by a crowd, and a man demanded money to convey our luggage to the hostel. This was provided for in the funds already paid, so I stoutly resisted the imposition. In the midst of the altercation I felt a hand gently tapping me on a shoulder, and, as I turned, Mr. Chapman said, "Pay the man the money."

Hotly I replied, "Indeed, Mr. Chapman, I shall not. Here is your purse, and you can do as you like, but I won't be taken in like that."

Never shall I forget the scene which followed. Quickly taking from his purse the amount demanded, Mr. Chapman took the man's hand in his, and, as he placed the money in it, told him he was quite aware that it was an imposition, but he had come to his country to tell the glad tidings of salvation, that "God so loved the world that He gave his only begotten Son." The money must have burned in the man's hand as he stood there and listened to the Gospel story.

A great change already began to pass through my mind as to the one who was my traveling companion, and instead of feeling my own importance as a great and accomplished traveler, I felt more as a child compared with him. After tea, Mr. Chapman asked if I would like a walk, to which I readily assented, and we spent some time together in passing from one part of the city to another.

Presently, Mr. Chapman turned to me with the question, "Brother, do you know the way back to our hotel?"

"Know my way back! Why no, Mr. Chapman; I have never been in this city before."

"Very well, then, let us ask God to guide us." Instantly, and before I had time to exclaim (which I did), I found myself drawn to the entrance of a side street, and heard Mr. Chapman in prayer, telling the Lord that we were in this city as His servants, and asking Him to guide us to the hotel, and to give us an opportunity of speaking to someone about his soul.

I was dumb. I knew nothing about this intimate intercourse and spirit of constant dependence upon God, and I just followed on. Presently, as we went down the street, Mr. Chapman, who had been scanning the names over the shops, stopped, and said, "That is an English name; let us go in."

It was a bell hanger's, and, as we entered, a man in a paper cap came out from an inside room. Going towards him, and holding out his hand, Mr. Chapman said, "You are English?"

"Yes, that I am, and right glad I am to hear my mother tongue. This is the first time since I came into this country any one has asked me such a question, or cared anything about me. If that is your errand, you had better come inside."

I followed, wondering what would come of it. Mr. Chapman's Bible was out at once, and soon a most interesting conversation over the Scriptures was going on. The man was deeply in earnest, and prayer followed. Then, rising from his knees, Mr. Chapman said, "We are strangers in the city; will you kindly direct us to our Hotel?"

"Direct you, sir; I'll go with you every step of the way," was the ready response, and did so, while I was deeply impressed with the character of the man of God into whose presence and companionship I had so unexpectedly been brought.

Years later, Chapman's traveling companion returned to Seville and located the bell hanger. As a result of his contact with Chapman, the bell hanger had been converted and was preaching the gospel!

In his later years, Chapman was blessed by positive spiritual changes in Spain. His trips had stimulated much missionary interest there; his constant prayers had helped open that country to the gospel. To those who had dedicated themselves to mission work in Spain and Portugal, he offered unfailing support. He prayed for these missionaries unceasingly. He constantly wrote them letters of encouragement. When visiting those countries, he worked with them side by side, distributing literature and preaching. When these missionaries returned to England on furlough, he offered them the opportunity to rest at his home.

Chapman counseled many prospective missionaries, including the young Hudson Taylor. Chapman greatly encouraged him to proceed with plans to evangelize in China. When Taylor set up the China Inland Mission, he named Chapman as one of the first "referees" of the mission. (Referees were supporters and advisors who would answer inquiries about the mission.)

Through the years, Taylor visited Chapman several times in Barnstaple. Chapman also encouraged Taylor through letters. One undated letter reads:

> My dear brother Taylor, consider our claim on you. We desire fellowship with you in your work. Oh! Come and speak to us your brethren here. Say when you can come.... God delights to fill our open mouths!

When they met again in 1872, Chapman greeted Taylor with the words, "I have visited you every day since you went to China," meaning he had prayed for Taylor daily.

Shortly after Chapman's death, J. Norman Case of the China Inland Mission wrote the following tribute. It aptly summarizes the fruit of Chapman's commitment to world missions.

> In him missionaries in China and other lands have lost a real friend and constant helper at the throne of grace.... It is truly marvellous how many lives were directed into and helped forward in paths of grace and godliness through the ministry and example of this one man. In Canada, in Australia, in China, as well as in many parts of the British Isles, we have met men and women who, in spite of opposition and scorn from friends, from professing Christians and the world, were pressing on in the...paths of New Testament church order, unworldly living, and self-denying service, largely nerved thereto by the consistent life of our departed friend.

## Thoughts for Meditation

*"I have great sorrow and unceasing grief in my heart. For I could wish that I myself were accursed, separated from Christ for the sake of my brethren, my kinsmen according to the flesh."*

Romans 9:2,3

*" 'The harvest is plentiful, but the laborers are few; therefore beseech the Lord of the harvest to send out laborers into His harvest.' "*

Luke 10:2

---

To a young missionary heading for the field Chapman said:

*"Keep low, look up, and press foreward."*

*"If we act only because our path is clear of difficulty, this is not Faith. Faith acts upon God's Word whatever the difficulty; and to walk by faith brings highest glory to God."*

R. C. C.

*"The chief excellency of Faith is that it brings us unto fellowship with God. Abel—the first spoken of in Hebrews 11—is commended, not because of any great deed on man's account, but because he worshipped God acceptably. Nevertheless, if we trust God, there is no limit to the power of Faith, whatever the thing to be done."*

R. C. C.

# Self-discipline

*"The fruit of the Spirit is love...[and] self-control."*

Galations 5:22a,23a

T he late Martyn Lloyd-Jones made this tremendously significant observation:

I defy you to read the life of any saint that has ever adorned the life of the Church without seeing at once that the greatest characteristic in the life of that saint was discipline and order. Invariably it is the universal characteristic of all the outstanding men and women of God.... Obviously it is something that is thoroughly scriptural and absolutely essential.[4]

Early in his ministry, Chapman recognized the vital need for an unfailing commitment to personal discipline. He saw great value in caring for his mind, body, and spirit. He saw the essential need for spiritual and physical refreshment, which was one reason why he provided a home of rest for Christian workers. His personal life was a model of disciplined Christian living that yielded spiritual fruit.

Chapman fed his spirit daily. He believed that because the Lord's servant is "continually ministering to others, he must be receiving fresh supplies from the God of all grace through all channels. Meditation on the Word and prayer should occupy the chief part of his time." On most days he read and meditated on God's Word for several hours. This time of study and fellowship with

God was the source of his spiritual strength as well as his personal knowledge of God's will. He also made prayer his constant business. He spoke to God about everything that was on his heart and would pray anytime, regardless of what activity he was doing.

Chapman was also very health conscious. To care for his physical body, Chapman usually went to bed early and got up early. He took long, vigorous walks each day. His long legs and rapid gait enabled him to cover great distances in a relatively short time, an ability that served him well during his missionary journeys. He ate simply and sparingly, and fasted on Saturday. Chapman often remarked that our bodies are to be used for God's service and that we must therefore take good care of them.

He gave equal care to his mental well-being. He firmly reserved each Saturday for himself, conducting no business and only seeing visitors in emergencies. His favorite spot for relaxing his mind and body in communion with God was a woodworking shop. Set up in a small room at the rear of his house, the shop contained a number of quality tools and a woodworking lathe. Through the years, he produced many fine pieces of furniture, making himself a desk and probably many other pieces. Some items were used in Bear Street Chapel; bowls and bread boards were given to some of his guests. He also sold some pieces to set up a fund for missionary support.

Although his commitments to his guests and the church at Barnstaple were important, Chapman did not allow them to usurp the personal disciplines that he knew he needed to follow. He knew the risks of failing to be disciplined in caring for himself. Therefore he consistently maintained these disciplines of spirit, mind, and body throughout his life. Even at age ninety-eight, one of Chapman's guests found him to be disciplined, enthusiastic, and mentally vigorous:

> On the Lord's Day, instead of appearing exhausted after his [Saturday] fast, at his advanced age, he seems fresher than ever. I heard him exclaim, with exuberant joyfulness, to one of his friends, "The Lord is risen indeed, my brother; the Lord is risen indeed!" He comes to breakfast on such

occasions with his soul filled and bubbling over with heavenly matters of praise and thanksgiving, which he pours into the ears and hearts of his listeners at the table. He is most entertaining, keeping up a genial and edifying conversation with his friends, and laughing very heartily when any amusing anecdote is related to him. . . . The beams from his cheerful countenance fall upon all alike, he having no favorites. "To have young brethren around me is one of my greatest comforts in my old age," he would often remark.

### *Thoughts for Meditation*

*"I buffet my body and make it my slave, lest possibly, after I have preached to others, I myself should be disqualified."*

1 Corinthians 9:27

*"Appoint elders in every city as I directed you, namely, if any man be . . . self-controlled."*

Titus 1:5b,6a,8b

---

*"God holds us accountable for what we have, and not for what we have not. If I have only ten minutes to read the Word, do I employ those ten minutes according to my accountability?"*

R. C. C.

*"Daniel made prayer and meditation of the Scriptures the chief business of his life; yet, if we consider the circumstances in which he was placed, we shall see that few ever had greater obstacles than he in the way of seeking God."*

R. C. C.

# Prayer and Worship

*"For he [Enoch] obtained the witness that before his being taken up he was pleasing to God."*

Hebrews 11:b

Above all else that we can say of Chapman, we can say that he was a godly man. For a Christian leader, there is no higher commendation. Ultimately, there is no greater power to move people for God than the example of a holy, godly life.

Like King David, Chapman loved to worship. He wrote some 165 hymns and poems. In sermons, meditations, and hymns, Chapman dwelt much on the Cross. That is one reason why he initiated, very early at Bear Street, a weekly Lord's Supper to keep Christ central and remember Him, "Who is our life." One of Chapman's best-known hymns expresses his deep thoughts of Christ's atoning work:

> O my Saviour crucified!
>     Near Thy cross would I abide;
> There to look, with steadfast eye,
>     On thy dying agony.
>
> Jesus, bruised and put to shame,
>     Tells me all Jehovah's name;
> "God is love," I surely know
>     By the Saviour's depths of woe.

> In His spotless soul's distress
> I perceive my guiltiness;
> Oh, how vile my low estate,
> Since my ransom was so great!
>
> Dwelling on Mount Calvary,
> Contrite shall my spirit be;
> Rest and holiness shall find,
> Fashioned like my Saviour's mind.

The Cross has great power to inspire love and devotion in us. Chapman said, "Would we be filled with love towards Christ—let us consider Christ's love towards us in the death of the Cross." A verse from another of his hymns expresses his well-known thirst for a greater knowledge of Christ's love:

> I would, my Lord and Saviour,
> Know that which no measure knows;
> Would search the mystery of Thy love,
> The depth of all Thy woes.

By 1837, Chapman had published a collection of his hymns, which the church at Barnstaple used for many years. Singing was an important part of worship at Bear Street Chapel. On Thursday nights there was singing practice at Chapman's home. Such practice greatly facilitated the Sunday-morning singing, especially teaching new songs to the congregation. Bear Street Chapel had become a mature, worshiping church.

Like all godly men, Chapman was a man of prayer. "If we have not the spirit of supplication and thanksgiving," he wrote, "let us begin with the spirit of confession." Chapman prayed about everything; no matter was too small for him to pray about. His delight in prayer overflowed into his hymns:

> O how I love in solitude,
> Great God, to speak with Thee,
> For Thou whose grace my soul renewed,
> A father art to me.

One of his favorite sayings was, "When I bow to God, God

stoops to me.'' Those who knew Chapman saw ample evidence of his confidence that God would stoop to him and listen to his prayers. Describing Chapman, a missionary acquaintance wrote:

> When first traveling in Spain, not knowing a single Christian in the whole country, he was not discouraged, but trusted in God. Years afterwards, when he saw the doors opened for the preaching of the Gospel. . .he was not in the least surprised; he had asked for it, and had patiently waited for the answer.

The following incident illustrates Chapman's dependence on God for protection during his missionary journeys.

> While I was walking along in a very lonely place in a certain part of Spain, two men came up behind me, and I heard them say, ''He is alone; let us rob him.'' I immediately lifted up my heart to God and sought deliverance; the answer came back at once, and the men left me without further annoyance.

Chapman's prayer life was by no means limited to praise and intercession for his personal needs. He regarded intercessory prayer for others as a special ministry: ''It is well for a child of God to pray for himself, but a more excellent thing to pray for others. God honours the spirit of intercession.''

And pray for others he did. One day, a woman he knew asked him to pray for her children. He replied, in his characteristic manner, ''I cannot begin to pray for your dear children.'' Startled, she began to apologize for imposing, but Chapman quickly interrupted her by saying, ''I cannot begin because I have already begun!''

In another instance, a young woman who felt called to work with children in Spain sought his counsel before making the journey. She knew of his work in Spain and his longstanding influence among missionaries there. Chapman spoke with her at his home in Barnstaple and asked her to return to him the next morning, which she did. At that time he gave her his approval and blessing, and prayed with her for her safety in the work to which God had called her.

While Chapman was praying, the cab arrived to take the young woman to the railway station. Although she heard the cab, she didn't interrupt Chapman's lengthy prayer. The cab waited for her, but she did not arrive at the station in time to catch her train. She later learned that the train had been in a serious accident and considered the incident to be a confirmation of God's provision for her safety. So she went to Spain, confident of God's leading.

With no desire to become an old man who mourned lost opportunities or looked back at what might have been, Chapman determined to live for Christ as long as he was able. In his later years, he accomplished that goal through fervent, intercessory prayer. Considering intercession to be "my chief business now," he spent much time in prayer, and requests came to him from around the world.

Chapman's holy life made a tremendous impact on people. Even those who had little use for God referred to him as a man of God or "that holy man." Many people believed that God especially protected him. Once, when he boarded a coach, the coachman announced, "You need not insure your lives today, gentlemen; Mr. Chapman is going with us." Another time, as the train on which he was riding descended the steep hill into Barnstaple, a woman panicked. The coachman assured her that there was no danger because Mr. Chapman was on the train.

People who held opposing theological views from Chapman still respected him. A local Roman Catholic, for example, was intent on convincing a visitor that all Protestants were lost because they were outside the true church. In the middle of his argument, he paused and added, "Well, there is one [Protestant] in Barnstaple who will get to heaven if anyone will. . . . I don't know his name, but he lives on New Buildings Street. He is the oldest and holiest man in Barnstaple."

Chapman delivered his last sermon at Grosvenor Chapel just before his ninety-eighth birthday. It lasted an hour and a quarter. On his ninety-ninth birthday, in January, 1902, he received congratulatory messages from all over the world. A reporter for the Barnstaple newspaper wrote a long article for that occasion, ending it with: "And not the least of Barnstaple's claims to distinction is that she has identified with the unique life-work of this scholar, saint, author, and preacher.'' Chapman spent his birthday simply, using a great part of it to make several platters to give to friends.

Several months later, on June 12, 1902, Robert Cleaver Chapman, beloved of God, went to be with his Lord.

Although Chapman avoided publicity and did nothing to seek fame, he became one of the most respected Christians of his time.

To many who had suggested that his life's work be written while he was still among his beloved people, he only replied that ''it was being written and would be published in the morning.'' Because he wanted people to dwell on their Savior, not on his life, Chapman purposely destroyed almost all of the letters he had received. Thus far less is known and written about him than about most of his contemporaries.

However, we do know that from his early twenties onward, Chapman's goal was ''to live Christ.'' How successful was he? Listen to Mr. J. R. Caldwell of Scotland as he reminisces over a visit Chapman made to his family when Chapman was in his eighties:

> Truly the memory of his visit remains with us as a precious illustration of how far God can reproduce in a believer even here the image of His Son.

Although Chapman wanted no one to revere him, his love touched so many people that fame became his legacy. Charles H. Spurgeon called him ''the saintliest man I ever knew.'' By the end of his life, Chapman was known worldwide for his love, wisdom, and compassion. He had become so well known in England that a letter from abroad addressed only to ''R. C. Chapman, University of Love, England,'' was correctly delivered to him!

## Notes

1. Michael Green, *Called to Serve*, "Christian Foundation" (Philadelphia: The Westminster Press, 1964), page 16.

2. "America's Southern Baptists," *Christianity Today* (November 4, 1988):29.

3. Paul E. Billheimer, *Love Covers* (Fort Washington, Pennsylvania: Christian Literature Crusade, 1981), page 34.

4. D. Martyn Lloyd-Jones, *Spiritual Depression* (Grand Rapids: Wm. B. Eerdmans Publishing Company, 1965), page 210.